Business English Vocabulary Builder:

Idioms, Phrases, and Expressions in American English

Jackie Bolen

1

2

Table of Contents

Introduction

Welcome to this book designed to help you improve your business English vocabulary with helpful idioms, phrases, and expressions in American English. My goal is to help you expand your business English vocabulary and to be able to speak and write more fluently.

Let's face it, business idioms can be difficult to master, even for the best students. In this book, you'll find more than three hundred business English idioms and phrases that are used in boardrooms, over lunch, at conferences and in offices around the world.

The best way to learn new vocabulary is in context. That's why each idiom and expression is introduced though a realistic dialogue. Then, you'll find a simple explanation for each one and then have a chance to put into practice what you've learned. Answers are included so that you can easily check your progress.

To get the most value from this book, be sure to do the following:

– Review frequently.

– Use each idiom or phrase in real life as soon as possible.

– Don't be nervous about making mistakes. That's how you'll get better at English.

– Do the practice sections. Try not to cheat and look at the answers too much!

– Consider studying with a friend to help each other stay motivated.

Good luck and I wish you well on your journey to become more proficient with business English.

About the Author: Jackie Bolen

I taught English in South Korea for 10 years to every level and type of student. I've taught every age from kindergarten kids to adults. Most of my time was centered around teaching at two universities: five years at a science and engineering school in Cheonan, and four years at a major university in Busan where I taught upper-level classes for students majoring in English. In my spare time, you can usually find me outside surfing, biking, hiking, or snowshoeing. I now live in Vancouver, Canada.

In case you were wondering what my academic qualifications are, I hold a Master of Arts in Psychology. During my time in Korea, I completed both the Cambridge CELTA and DELTA certification programs. With the combination of almost ten years teaching ESL/EFL learners of all ages and levels, and the more formal teaching qualifications I've obtained, I have a solid foundation on which to offer advice to English learners.

I truly hope that you find this book useful. I would love it if you sent me an email with any questions or feedback that you might have.

Jackie Bolen (www.jackiebolen.com)

Twitter: @bolen_jackie

Email: jb.business.online@gmail.com

You might also be interested in this book: _Advanced English Conversation Dialogues_ by Jackie Bolen. It has hundreds of helpful English idioms and expressions that can be used in a wide variety of situations to help you learn to speak more fluently in American English.

Disagreeing with a Decision

Jerry: I don't want to **make waves** here, but I don't think Kim is making a good financial decision for our company.

Linda: Oh, I don't know. Maybe you just don't see **eye to eye**? I think she's done a lot of research and **knows what she's doing**. She's generally quite good at making decisions. It's why they pay her the **big bucks**.

Jerry: Well, I understand why you'd think that. You were **born with a silver spoon in your mouth**, just like Kim, and have never really been **short on cash**. Anyway, it's some **food for thought**!

Linda: To play the **Devil's advocate**, making big decisions is **second nature** to her. She's great at it!

Jerry: Hmmm...okay. Let's **agree to disagree**. We're never going to **settle** this I think.

Vocabulary

See eye to eye: Agree with someone.

Born with a silver spoon in your mouth: Someone who comes from a wealthy family who doesn't have to work that hard in life.

Food for thought: Something to think about.

Make waves: To cause trouble.

Devil's advocate: Someone who takes the other side in an argument.

Knows what she's doing: Sure of something or do something correctly.

Agree to disagree: To stop talking about something controversial when you can't agree.

Settle: Decide or agree to something.

Big bucks: To have a very high salary.

Second Nature: Something that someone does easily and well because they have done it so often.

6

Exercise

Fill in the blanks with the correct phrase or idiom.

1. My mom and I had to finally _____ because there was no way we could understand each other's point of view.
2. I'm not trying to _____ but I just don't agree with what's going on at my company.
3. I'm thinking about changing jobs. My boss and I don't _____.
4. My cousin was _____ and has never had to work a day in his life.
5. My younger brother's most annoying habit is his need to always play the _____.
6. That newspaper article had some _____ in it.
7. I've learned so much from my teacher. I can see she _____.
8. I was hoping to not have to _____ for that job because the salary isn't great but it's tough in this economy.
9. Skating is _____ to him. He's been doing it since he was three.
10. He has a ton of responsibility but that's why they pay him the _____.

Answers:

1. agree to disagree
2. make waves
3. see eye to eye
4. born with a silver spoon in his mouth
5. Devil's advocate
6. food for thought
7. knows what she's doing
8. settle
9. second nature
10. big bucks

Asking for Clarification

Harper: Just so I'm clear on this: you're asking me to **scale back** production on Model 1234?

Logan: Yes, correct. Fuel prices are **skyrocketing** and there isn't as much demand for things that aren't fuel-efficient. Put it on the **backburner** for now.

Harper: Is this the plan **for the long haul**?

Logan: **Pretty much** as long as fuel prices remain at current levels and we're **in the red**. We're **feeling the pinch** with our expansion into Canada and we just don't have **money to burn** like we did a few years ago.

Harper: Okay, I got it. I'll let my team know.

Vocabulary:

Scale back: Reduce something.

Skyrocketing: Increasing rapidly

Backburner: Leave something for now and deal with it later.

For the long haul: For the long term.

Pretty much: Almost 100% certain.

In the red: Losing money.

Feeling the pinch: Experiencing financial difficulties.

Money to burn: Extra money to spend freely.

Exercise:

Fill in the blanks with the correct phrase or idiom.

1. Look at that new car he bought. He must have _____.

2. My company is in it _____.

3. I'm worried about this project that's now running _____.

4. We're _____ with Covid-19.

5. I _____ only want to know where I stand with this company.

6. Let's put this on the _____ until the economy recovers.

7. Fuel prices are _____ these days with the shortages.

8. Let's _____ production until the new model comes out.

Answers:

1. money to burn

2. for the long haul

3. in the red

4. feeling the pinch

5. pretty much

6. backburner

7. skyrocketing

8. scale back

Talking about Co-workers

Jerry: Why are all of our co-workers **living hand to mouth**? We get paid a **living wage. I can't make heads or tails of it**.

Linda: Well, I think most of them **hit the bottle** pretty hard after work every day. That **costs a pretty penny**. But, your **guess is as good as mine**.

Jerry: **Come to think of it,** I've noticed that too. I used to **drink a lot** but now it's only **once in a blue moon**. I **quit cold turkey** for a couple of years before I could **get a handle on it**.

Linda: Good for you for making a big change like that! Plus, it's saved you a lot of money I'm sure. Don't **blow it all** on stuff that isn't long-lasting, right?

Vocabulary

Once in a blue moon: Something that doesn't happen often.

Quit cold turkey: Suddenly stop doing something addictive. Most commonly refers to smoking.

Living hand to mouth: To live paycheck to paycheck. Not having lots of money, especially disposable income.

Living wage: Salary that is high enough to cover all the monthly bills relatively easily.

Your guess is as good as mine: To not know something.

Hit the bottle: Drink alcohol.

Get a handle on it: To control something.

Costs a pretty penny: Is expensive.

Can't make heads or tails of it: Unable to understand something.

Drink a lot: Consume lots of alcohol.

Come to think of it: On reflection after hearing someone say something about it.

Blow it all: To waste everything, usually money.

Exercise

Fill in the blanks with the correct phrase or idiom.

1. My dad _____ hard when I was a kid.
2. That new car I want _____.
3. I'm going back to school so can find a job that pays a _____.
4. I only eat junk food _____.
5. I want to quit smoking but it's difficult to _____.
6. I've heard that the best way to stop smoking is to _____.
7. It's often hard for single parents to avoid _____.
8. Math just isn't my subject! I _____.
9. Wow! They sure do _____.
10. _____, that was a strange decision Tim made.
11. I'm worried about my Dad and his big pension payout. I think he might _____ on junk.

Answers:

1. hit the bottle
2. costs a pretty penny
3. living wage
4. once in a blue moon
5. get a handle on it
6. quit cold turkey
7. living hand to mouth
8. can't make heads or tails of it
9. drink a lot
10. come to think of it
11. blow it all.

Talking about a Customer

Emma: Hey, so I was just talking to Noah and it looks like they won't renew the contract. It's a bit **up in the air** but I think they want to **sever ties** with us.

Oliver: To me, **the writing is on the wall**. They haven't been happy for months now.

Emma: Not to **throw someone under the bus** but the **elephant in the room** is Mia's performance as their account manager. It's just not good enough.

Oliver: I think you've **hit the nail on the head**. She's already **in the dog house** with that other account she manages.

Emma: She's **all talk**. It's time she **puts her money where her mouth is**.

Oliver: I'd love to go behind her back and **blow the whistle** on this but I don't want to draw attention to myself.

Vocabulary:

Up in the air: Not decided yet.

Sever ties: To stop a relationship.

The writing is on the wall: It's obvious to everyone.

Throw someone under the bus: To blame someone for something.

The elephant in the room: The obvious thing that nobody is talking about.

Hit the nail on the head: See the problem clearly.

In the dog house: In trouble.

All talk: Good at talking but their actions don't reflect this.

Puts her money where her mouth is: Her actions need to reflect her words.

Blow the whistle: To disclose true information that might be harmful to someone.

Exercise:

Fill in the blanks with the correct phrase or idiom.

1. Honestly, I just think he should _____ on his company. They're doing some terrible things.

2. I'm _____ with my kids if I get home too late from work.

3. I think we need to _____ with that contractor.

4. Why is nobody talking about _____?

5. It's time for her to _____ and do some work.

6. He's _____ but no action.

7. I hate that we have to _____ for this.

8. You've made a good point and _____ exactly.

9. Don't you think that _____? I'm going to get fired.

10. I don't think she's made the decision yet. It's still _____.

Answers:

1. blow the whistle

2. in the dog house

3. sever ties

4. the elephant in the room

5. put her money where her mouth is

6. all talk

7. throw someone under the bus

8. hit the nail on the head

9. the writing is on the wall

10. up in the air

Talking about a New Co-worker

Jerry: Have you met our new co-worker yet?

Linda: I talked to him yesterday but he's **a hard nut to crack**. He only gave one-word answers to all my questions! He seems to keep everyone **at arm's length**.

Jerry: Well, **you can't judge a book by its cover**. I'm sure we'll find out more about him as time goes on. Maybe he's not that **talkative.**

Linda: Maybe. But I felt frustrated talking to him for just a few minutes. Anyway, I'm working on not **burning bridges** so I'll **put my best foot forward**!

Jerry: Good plan. You never know **what may come**. **It's a long shot**, but let's invite him out for lunch and see if he **opens up**.

Linda: **My gut tells me** that we just **got off on the wrong foot**. Let's see!

Vocabulary

You can't judge a book by its cover: To not judge something or someone based on appearance. For example, a restaurant that's not stylish may have delicious food.

A hard nut to crack: Someone that is difficult to get to know.

At arm's length: Avoids being close with people.

Burning bridges: Damaging relationships.

Put my best foot forward: To be on one's best behaviour.

What may come: What could happen in the future.

Talkative: Describes someone who likes to talk a lot.

It's a long shot: Something that's not likely to happen.

Opens up: Shares information about oneself.

My gut tells me: Instinct or intuition about someone or something.

Got off on the wrong foot: A bad first meeting or start to something.

Exercise

Fill in the blanks with the correct phrase or idiom.

1. _____ to not hire that guy. I'm not sure why but it just seems like a bad decision.
2. I know _____ but I hope to win that contract.
3. I try to avoid _____ when I leave a job. Who knows what the future holds.
4. That client is _____.
5. My new co-worker is so _____ that I have a difficult time getting any work done!
6. My boss and I _____ but we're doing okay now.
7. I hope that my client _____ to me more about what his company is going through right now. I think I can offer him some assistance.
8. I'm not sure _____ but I want to be prepared for all the possibilities.
9. I always try to _____ when starting a new job.
10. I feel like my boss is keeping me _____. I'm not sure why.
11. Over the years I've learned that _____.

Answers:

1. my gut tells me
2. it's a long shot
3. burning bridges
4. a hard nut to crack
5. talkative
6. got off on the wrong foot
7. opens up
8. what may come
9. put my best foot forward
10. at arm's length
11. you can't judge a book by its cover

Talking about Someone Who Got Fired

Jerry: Did you hear that Beth **got canned** last month?

Linda: Oh wow! **No kidding**.

Jerry: It turned out to be a **blessing in disguise** though. She got a higher-paying job **in no time.**

Linda: Oh, that's great. She wasn't **living within her means**, **splashing out** all the time. Maybe this will solve her **financial woes**. Give me a **ballpark figure**. How much?

Jerry: **Time will tell** about solving her financial woes. I'll have to **see it to believe it.** I think she's making around $100,000 now.

Linda: Well, at least she gets to start with a **clean slate**. It's a good opportunity for her.

Vocabulary

Blessing in Disguise: Something that initially seems bad which turns out good in the end. For example, someone lost their job but ended up getting a better job three months later.

Living within her means: To not spend more than she makes.

Got canned: Fired from a job.

No kidding: A response to something surprising.

In no time: Quickly.

Splashing out: Spending extravagantly.

Financial woes: Money trouble.

Time will tell: Wait and see.

See it to believe it: When you don't think something is likely.

Clean slate: New beginning.

Ballpark figure: Rough estimate.

Exercise

Fill in the blanks with the correct phrase or idiom.

1. Be patient. _____ if that was a good decision or not.
2. Do you honestly think that he's changed? I'll have to _____.
3. Wow, _____. I can't believe I won the contest!
4. My brother _____ because he was always late for work.
5. Are you sure you want to buy me dinner? You're really _____.
6. Maybe getting fired was a _____. I hated that job.
7. I'm trying to teach my wife about _____ but it's an uphill battle.
8. Just let me know a _____ for how much this going to cost.
9. I'm embarrassed to admit it, but all of our _____ were caused by me.
10. I had the project done _____ but my boss still wasn't satisfied.
11. I love changing jobs! It's like starting with a _____.

Answers:

1. Time will tell
2. see it to believe it
3. no kidding
4. got canned
5. splashing out
6. blessing in disguise
7. living within her means
8. ballpark figure
9. financial woes
10. in no time
11. clean slate

Small Talk at Work #1

Jerry: I'm thinking about running a marathon. I have **butterflies in my stomach** though. It's going to be difficult!

Linda: What? It'll be **a piece of cake** for you. You're **as fit as a fiddle**.

Jerry: I know I'm always **cool as a cucumber** when I start the race but then I get so tired in the middle. I eventually get a **second wind** though.

Linda: **Fingers crossed** that you'll **knock 'em dead**. I'll come to cheer for you!

Jerry: What about you? Did the doctor give you **a clean bill of health**? You can train with me.

Linda: I'm not quite **back on my feet** yet. Plus, I have **a lot on my plate** right now. I've been **working day and night** on this latest project. I need **a change of pace** for sure!

Vocabulary

A piece of cake: Something that's easy to do.

Cool as a cucumber: Very calm or relaxed.

As fit as a fiddle: In really good shape.

Second wind: Having some energy again after being tired. Usually applies to exercise or staying up late.

Butterflies in my stomach: Nervous feeling about something.

Fingers crossed: To wish someone good luck. Or, a symbol of good luck.

Knock 'em dead: Do well or be successful at an event.

A clean bill of health: Healthy, not sick anymore.

Back on my feet: Recovered, after a problem (health, financial, divorce, etc.)

A lot on my plate: Many responsibilities.

Working day and night: Working all the time.

A change of pace: Something new or different.

Exercise

Fill in the blanks with the correct phrase or idiom.

1. Don't worry, I'm sure you'll _____.
2. Under pressure, Roger Federer is as _____.
3. I always get _____ before a test.
4. That speaking test was _____.
5. I've got my _____ waiting for the results of the SAT.
6. My grandpa is _____ even though he is 80.
7. My wife has been _____ to get the latest project done at work.
8. I hope I get my _____. I have lots more studying to do!
9. I'm hoping to get _____ after my recent job loss.
10. I'm moving to Costa Rica for _____.
11. I'm hoping that the doctors give me _____.
12. I'm going to have _____ this week at work.

Answers:

1. knock 'em dead
2. cool as a cucumber
3. butterflies in my stomach
4. a piece of cake
5. fingers crossed
6. as fit as a fiddle
7. working day and night
8. second wind
9. back on my feet
10. a change of pace
11. a clean bill of health
12. a lot of my plate

19

Small Talk at Work #2

Jerry: To **add insult to injury**, my dad got Covid-19 when he was in the hospital with a heart attack.

Linda: Oh no. Is he okay?

Jerry: Well, he's not **out of the woods** yet. He's still **sick as a dog** but he's not **at death's door**. He does need **round the clock** care though.

Linda: Send him my **best wishes**, okay? And **keep me updated** on how he's doing.

Jerry: **Don't waste your breath**. He still acts like he got up on the **wrong side of the bed** all the time. We've **never seen eye to eye**.

Linda: Well, you certainly don't **take after** him. Don't worry!

Vocabulary

Add insult to Injury: Make something already bad worse. For example, a guy fell off his bike but then a car ran over his foot.

Out of the woods: A difficult situation that has improved. Usually refers to medical things when someone is very sick but has recovered a little bit.

Don't waste your breath: Whatever you say doesn't make a difference.

Sick as a dog: Very unwell.

Round the clock: All day, every day.

At death's door: Close to dying.

Keep me updated: To ask someone to tell you what's happening with a situation.

Wrong side of the bed: Grumpy.

Best wishes: Friendly hope that someone is doing well.

Take after: Usually a son/daughter who is similar to his/her mother/father.

Never seen eye to eye: Never agreed.

Exercise

Fill in the blanks with the correct phrase or idiom.

1. My sister hates mornings and often gets up on the _____.

2. I was _____ last year and spent a week in the hospital.

3. He's doing better but he's not _____ yet.

4. I can't believe he made it! He was _____.

5. _____. I've already made up my mind.

6. I honestly don't want to _____ but it looks like you have a flat tire too.

7. I've been working _____ on this project at work. I'm so tired.

8. My boss and I have _____ on how to deal with that client.

9. _____ on your recent engagement!

10. Please _____ on whether or not you can get a hold of that client.

11. I hope my son doesn't _____ me. I haven't been the best example for him growing up.

Answers:

1. wrong side of the bed

2. sick as a dog

3. out of the woods

4. at death's door

5. Don't waste your breath

6. add insult to injury

7. never seen eye to eye

8. round the clock

9. best wishes

10. keep me updated

11. take after

Small Talk at Work #3

Tim: The weather looks great for the weekend. Do you have any plans?

Carrie: I'm going to get my garden ready for planting. I have **my work cut out for me**. It's so overgrown. But, it's not **set in stone**. I'll see what else comes up!

Tim: Yeah, it is that time of year, right? The days are getting longer. I'm going to **play it by ear**. Honestly, I'm pretty **burned out** and am **barely treading water**. The **fallout** from the **cost-cutting measures** has had a huge impact on me.

Carrie: Sorry to hear that. Is there anything I can do to help?

Tim: Nah, it's okay. Gotta **bring home the bacon**, right? It's not all **doom and gloom**. I may **rally the troops** for a movie or something.

Carrie: You **got hit hard by** that. Don't you want to **throw in the towel?**

Vocabulary

My work cut out for me: A big or difficult job to do.

Set in stone: Decided 100%.

Burned out: Tired, stressed and overworked.

Treading water: Barely keeping up with work or school.

Fallout: Negative consequences.

Cost-cutting measures: Something done to save money.

Bring home the bacon: Make money with a job.

Doom and gloom: Only bad things.

Rally the troops: Organize or convince people to do something.

Got hit hard by: To be badly affected by something.

Throw in the towel: To quit or give up.

Exercise

Fill in the blanks with the correct phrase or idiom.

1. Okay, who's going to _____ to check out that new Chinese place for lunch?
2. I'm barely _____ at my new job and am worried that I'll get fired.
3. We're not the only ones who _____ by Covid-19.
4. I hate my job but someone has to _____.
5. It's not all _____. He did get a B+ in English.
6. I have _____ with this new team.
7. I quit that job because I was so _____.
8. The _____ went too far I think. We're so understaffed now.
9. Nobody anticipated this would be the _____ from that decision.
10. Someone has to get fired but nothing is _____.
11. I'm ready to _____ on that project! It's brought me nothing but grief.

Answers:

1. rally the troops
2. treading water
3. got hit hard by
4. bring home the bacon
5. doom and gloom
6. my work cut out for me
7. burned out
8. cost-cutting measures
9. fallout
10. set in stone
11. throw in the towel

Talking about the New Coffee Machine

Tim: Hey Carrie! I was supposed to **keep this under wraps** but Tony **splashed out** and we're getting a new espresso machine.

Carrie: Seriously? I've been bugging Tony about that for years now! I can't believe he finally **caved in**. **My lips are sealed**.

Tim: I know, right? It's coming next week. It's nice to **have your voice heard**.

Carrie: Wow! Work just got a whole lot better. The coffee machine now is seriously **below par.** If they want us to **burn the candle at both ends**, there's gotta be some perks.

Tim: I think Tony got a bit of a **reality check** when Min-Ji quit. He had to **step up to the plate** to keep the rest of us happy.

Vocabulary

Keep this under wraps: Not tell anyone about it.

Splashed out: Spent a lot of money.

Caved in: Finally agreed to something.

My lips are sealed: A promise to not tell anyone.

Have your voice heard: Someone listens to you.

Below par: Not good enough.

Burn the candle at both ends: Work very hard from early morning to late at night.

Reality check: Reminder about how things really are.

Step up to the plate: Take responsibility.

Exercise

Fill in the blanks with the correct phrase or idiom.

1. If he doesn't want to get fired, he's going to need to _____.

2. His performance this quarter was _____.

3. I finally _____ and gave her that day off she requested.

4. Johnny losing his job was a bit of a _____ for me.

5. I'm going to tell you who we decided to hire but please _____.

6. It sounds like you need to _____ at work.

7. I don't want to _____ for much longer. I need to find a new job.

8. Tell me your secret! _____.

9. My Dad really _____ for Christmas this year and took us all to Hawaii.

Answers:

1. step up to the plate

2. below par

3. caved in

4. reality check

5. keep this under wraps

6. have your voice heard

7. burn the candle at both ends

8. my lips are sealed

9. splashed out

Motivating Employees

Brendan: So I'm just going to **cut to the chase** here. We're **getting some heat** from management. Our results this quarter aren't great. We need to stay more **on top of things** and **keep our eyes on the prize,** which is sales.

Riley: Thanks for **bringing us up to speed**. I had a feeling that our numbers weren't going to be great. We spent a ton of time **troubleshooting** that bug in the reporting software.

Brendan: I know, you did a great job **thinking outside the box** on that issue. You **headed it off at the pass** and it could have been way worse.

Riley: Sales will be on my mind **24-7**. I want to get **ahead of the pack** and exceed targets.

Brendan: Great. It sounds like we're on the same page. No more deals can **fall through**.

Vocabulary

Cut to the chase: Get to the main point.

Getting some heat: Feeling some pressure.

On top of things: Organized.

Keep our eyes on the prize: Remember the most important thing.

Bringing us up to speed: Updating.

Troubleshooting: Finding and fixing the problem.

Thinking outside the box: Creative thinking about something.

Headed it off at the pass: Stopped something from becoming worse.

24-7 (twenty-four-seven): All day, every day.

Ahead of the pack: To be in front of competitors.

Fall through: Something that didn't work out.

Exercise

Fill in the blanks with the correct phrase or idiom.

1. I'm a bit worried that this deal is going to _____.

2. Thanks for _____ on this new project.

3. It's on my mind _____.

4. I want to get _____ so let's get down to work!

5. I'm not going to waste your time and I'll just _____ here.

6. Braden is good at _____.

7. Elissa did a nice job with that malfunction and _____.

8. We've been _____ from the big boss!

9. Let's focus on _____.

10. This new problem will require some serious _____.

11. I'm hoping we can stay _____ and not get behind on this project.

Answers:

1. fall through

2. bringing us up to speed

3. 24-7

4. ahead of the pack

5. cut to the chase

6. thinking outside the box

7. headed it off at the pass

8. getting some heat

9. keeping our eyes on the prize

10. troubleshooting

11. on top of things

Introducing Someone Making a Presentation

Brendan: Today I'd like to introduce our presenter, Chloe Stevenson. **From day one** at our company, she's **made an impact**. She got our ABC accounting software **up and running from the ground up.** Her implementation of this new software has been right **on the money** and **across the board**, we feel lucky to have her on our team! Honestly, I'm a bit **out of my depth** when it comes to the ins and outs of this stuff, so we'll let Chloe get to it! Welcome, and I hope everyone enjoys the presentation.

Chloe: Thanks Brendan, you certainly helped me **get started off on the right foot** here. Hopefully, it'll be **smooth sailing** from here on out!

Vocabulary

From day one: Since the beginning.

Made an impact: Made a difference, usually in a good way.

Up and running: To get something started.

From the ground up: From the beginning.

On the money: Correct thinking or action.

Across the board: Applies to everyone.

Out of my depth: Not qualified for, lack knowledge of.

Get started off on the right foot: Make a good beginning to something.

Smooth sailing: Goes well.

Exercise

Fill in the blanks with the correct phrase or idiom.

1. I hope it's going to be _____. I don't have much time to work on this.
2. Tom _____ when he started that new role.
3. I hope to _____ at this new job.
4. His advice was _____.
5. I'm worried that I'm going to be _____ on this project.
6. I think we need to overhaul this team, _____.
7. _____, we think that Tim needs to get fired.
8. _____, he's never been a good fit at this company.
9. She's done a great job at getting this new software _____.

Answers:

1. smooth sailing
2. made an impact
3. get started off on the right foot
4. on the money
5. out of my depth
6. from the ground up
7. across the board
8. from day one
9. up and running

Asking for Time Off

Bob: Hey Linda, I'd like to talk to you about taking some time off. I hoped to **get the ball rolling ahead of time** on this.

Linda: Oh, you've **caught me off guard**! But, what days would you like?

Bob: Well, I just found out my ex-wife's plans for this summer so I'd love to take the kids on vacation the first two weeks of July.

Linda: Hmmm...that's when everyone wants vacation time. But since you're the first to ask me, let's cut through all the **red tape**. I'll approve it, but **mum's the word**, okay?

Bob: Of course, thank you!

Linda: I don't want to be the **bad guy**, you know? Thanks for being so **on the ball** with this.

Vocabulary

Get the ball rolling: Start or begin something.

Ahead of time: Doing something earlier than required?

Caught me off guard: Surprised me.

Red tape: Unnecessary or restrictive rules or regulations.

Mum's the word: Don't tell anyone.

Bad guy: A person not well-liked.

On the ball: Organized.

Exercise

Fill in the blanks with the correct phrase or idiom.

1. I wish my boss was more _____ with assigning vacation time.
2. I'm just hoping to _____ on this before it's too late.
3. Oh! I'm not sure about that. You _____.
4. I hate to be the _____ here, but this project won't get done by itself.
5. I love to get things done _____ so I can have less stress at work.
6. I'll tell you but _____, okay?
7. When I take over, I want to cut through all the _____.

Answers:

1. on the ball
2. get the ball rolling
3. caught me off guard
4. bad guy
5. ahead of time
6. mum's the word
7. red tape

Getting Back to Work

Tim: So, I think I need to get back to work.

Carrie: You **beat me to the punch**. That newsletter isn't getting written by itself. I've been **burning the midnight oil** working on this thing.

Tim: I know, right? Same with my report. It was nice to **bounce some ideas off of you**.

Carrie: Same here. We sure do **bend over backwards** for this place!

Tim: Anything to **earn a living**, right? I don't mind **going the extra mile**. We get treated pretty well. Let's **get down to business**!

Vocabulary

Beat me to the punch: Say or do something before someone else.

Burning the midnight oil: Working very long hours, late into the night.

Bounce some ideas off of you: To talk about ideas informally.

Bend over backwards: Work extra hard.

Earn a living: Work at a job.

Going the extra mile: Working very hard to do a good job.

Get down to business: Start working (again).

Exercise

Fill in the blanks with the correct phrase or idiom.

1. I was going to take credit for that but Jenny _____.
2. Let's _____. Time is not on our side.
3. He did his job but he hated _____.
4. I'm hoping you have some time this week. I'd like to _____.
5. I've been _____ trying to finish up this presentation.
6. There must be an easier way to _____.
7. My boss expects me to _____ for her. I don't mind once in a while but it's all the time.

Answers:

1. beat me to the punch
2. get down to business
3. going the extra mile
4. bounce some ideas off of you
5. burning the midnight oil
6. earn a living
7. bend over backwards

Considering a Job Change

Jerry: I want to **nip this in the bud** now that the **cat's out of the bag**. I don't want people talking about me at work.

Linda: Oh, **spill the beans,** Jerry. I haven't heard anything about it.

Jerry: Well, I'm thinking about leaving the company but nothing is final yet. I do have some **irons in the fire** though. I don't want people talking about it because I may end up staying.

Linda: **Say no more**. **Your secret is safe with me**. I have a feeling that **the ball is in your court** though. You're the most qualified guy around here by a long shot.

Jerry: Thanks, Linda. I know that I **bring lots to the table** but **the bottom line** is who is going to pay me more!

Vocabulary

The cat's out of the bag: Accidentally reveal something secret.

Spill the beans: To tell a secret.

Nip this in the bud: To stop something bad from happening early on in the process.

Irons in the fire: A few different plans.

Say no more: The matter is finished or decided.

Your secret is safe with me: Not telling a secret to other people.

The ball is in your court: You have the power to decide on something.

Bring lots to the table: Have a lot of skills, money, wisdom, talent, etc.

The bottom line: The final outcome or thing to base a decision on.

Exercise

Fill in the blanks with the correct phrase or idiom.

1. _____. I'm on top of this right now.
2. I can tell you now that _____.
3. Doug and Jenny _____ and I'm happy that our company hired them.
4. I want to _____ before it becomes a much bigger issue.
5. Come on! Just _____, please!
6. My dad has so many _____ with all his side-gigs.
7. I think you can do whatever you want! _____ now.
8. Don't worry about it! _____.
9. Honestly, _____ is that I'm going to work for whoever pays me more.

Answers:

1. say no more
2. the cat's out of the bag
3. bring lots to the table
4. nip this in the bud
5. spill the beans
6. irons in the fire
7. the ball is in your court
8. your secret is safe with me
9. the bottom line

Disagreeing with a Co-worker

Jerry: I think I've found a way that I can **kill two birds with one stone** on this project at work. It's a little bit **sketchy** though. There's **a lot at stake**.

Linda: Oh Jerry, you know that stuff like that **isn't my cup of tea**. I like to keep everything **aboveboard** and hate these backroom deals.

Jerry: Yeah, I know. You're always on the **up and up**. But I don't mind **crossing the line** once in a while.

Linda: Well, keep me **out of the loop**! I don't want to hear any more about it.

Jerry: Okay, okay! I know you do everything **by the book**. I'll talk to Kenny about it. He likes to **think outside the box** about this kind of stuff.

Vocabulary

Kill two birds with one stone: Achieving two things with one single effort. For example, using the same essay for two different university classes.

Isn't my cup of tea: Not something I would do. For example, you have a friend who loves skydiving but you have no interest in it.

Up and up: Not illegal or sketchy.

Aboveboard: Not illegal or sketchy.

Crossing the line: Doing something illegal or not quite honest/right.

Out of the loop: Not knowing anything about something.

Sketchy: Not completely legal or right.

By the book: Completely legal, doing something the correct way.

Think outside the box: Think differently than most people would.

A lot at stake: There are important things that could be lost if something fails.

Backroom deals: Deals that happens secretly.

Exercise

Fill in the blanks with the correct phrase or idiom.

1. He's been _____ a lot lately. I'm not surprised that he finally got caught.
2. That popular new TV show just _____.
3. I remember him being pretty sketchy but he seems like he's on the _____ now.
4. Am I the only one who didn't know she was pregnant? I'm so _____.
5. I wish my company was a bit more _____. It's a bit difficult to work for them sometimes.
6. There's _____ with this upcoming work project.
7. I'm hoping to _____ to potentially save myself a lot of time.
8. My Internet provider seems a little bit _____ but I love how cheap they are.
9. One of the things that frustrates me about my wife is that she does everything completely _____.
10. Let's try to _____ about this problem.
11. To get things done in this industry, you have to make _____.

Answers:

1. crossing the line
2. isn't my cup of tea
3. up and up
4. out of the loop
5. aboveboard
6. a lot at stake
7. kill two birds with one stone
8. sketchy
9. by the book
10. think outside the box
11. backroom deals

Complaining about a Co-worker #1

Jerry: I'm ready to **blow a gasket**. Nobody wants to talk about **the elephant in the room**.

Linda: Oh yeah? What's going on?

Jerry: Well, the project manager at my company is not **on the ball.** We keep talking about budgets and timelines but this guy should **get canned.** Everything goes through him but it's like **pulling teeth**. It's like he's **at cross purposes** with everyone else on the project.

Linda: It sounds like you guys are **getting into deep water**. Will your client **bail**?

Jerry: I'm starting to wonder. If I was **in their shoes**, I'd certainly demand a change. They're **bleeding money** right now because of it. I know there's **a learning curve** but this is too much.

Linda: Tough times. I'm curious to see what happens.

Vocabulary

The elephant in the room: Something obvious and important that nobody wants to talk about.

On the ball: Easily understands things or reacts quickly to a situation.

Getting into deep water: To be in trouble.

Get canned: Get fired from a job.

Blow a gasket: Get very angry or annoyed.

Pulling teeth: Something painful or difficult to do.

Bail: To leave or exit quickly; to give up on something.

In their shoes: How you would act if you were in someone else's situation.

Bleeding money: Losing money very quickly.

At cross purposes: Having different goals from each other.

A learning curve: Time it takes to figure out something new.

Exercise

Fill in the blanks with the correct phrase or idiom.

1. Honestly, my job would be decent if the company wasn't _____.
2. It's time to _____! I'm nervous that someone is going to call the police.
3. There's _____ for this new software and I'm having a difficult time.
4. My brother might _____ because he's always leaving early.
5. Everyone is beating around the bush talking about unimportant stuff. But, I wish I had enough courage to mention _____.
6. He's _____ with all his financial commitments.
7. My boss is _____, unlike the last guy.
8. My boss and I are _____ on this latest project and it's so frustrating.
9. My dad is usually a pretty relaxed guy but sometimes he'd _____ over something minor.
10. It's honestly like _____ to get any information out of him.
11. Before judging, try to put yourself _____.

Answers:

1. bleeding money
2. bail
3. a learning curve
4. get canned
5. the elephant in the room
6. getting into deep water
7. on the ball
8. at cross purposes
9. blow a gasket
10. pulling teeth
11. in their shoes

Complaining about a Co-worker 2

Jerry: I just had a big fight with my friend and I'm not sure I can just **get over it.** It was a **massive blow-up.**

Linda: Oh no! What happened?

Jerry: Well, she's my co-worker and keeps **stealing my thunder** on work projects. She's taking credit for stuff that I do. I'm **sick and tired of it.** I just caught her **red-handed**.

Linda: That's a **tough pill to swallow**. I'd for sure have a **bee in my bonnet** about this too.

Jerry: It's not even **the straw that broke the camel's back.** She owes me a thousand **bucks** as well.

Linda: Honestly, she sounds like a **bad egg.**

Vocabulary

Stealing my thunder: Taking credit for something that someone else did.

Get over it: To fully recover (from an illness) or not think about it negatively anymore (break-up with a girlfriend or boyfriend, losing a job, etc.).

Tough pill to swallow: Something difficult to get over.

Bee in my bonnet: A certain issue that is annoying someone.

The straw that broke the camel's back: The last thing in a series of bad things before an event occurs — like a breakup, quitting a job, or fight.

Blow-up: Big fight or problem.

Massive: Very big/huge.

Sick and tired of it: Annoyed by something that happens frequently.

Bucks: Dollars.

Red-handed: Caught doing something bad.

Bad egg: A bad or dishonest person.

Exercise

Fill in the blanks with the correct phrase or idiom.

1. He looks like a million _____ these days.

2. I get a _____ any time I deal with that certain customer at work.

3. My mom is pretty relaxed but she would have a big _____ every once in a while.

4. Tony got fired after his boss caught him stealing _____.

5. He got a _____ raise at work. Lucky guy!

6. My teammate keeps _____ and always seems to forget that I set him up for most of his goals.

7. Getting a D on that test was a _____.

8. I can't just _____. I'm still in love with my ex-boyfriend.

9. That last project was _____ before I quit.

10. My mom is _____. She's gone on strike!

11. One _____ can negatively influence an entire company.

Answers:

1. bucks

2. bee in my bonnet

3. blow-up

4. red-handed

5. massive

6. stealing my thunder

7. tough pill to swallow

8. get over it

9. the straw that broke the camel's back

10. sick and tired of it

11. bad egg

Talking about Conflict at Work

Jerry: Oh wow. I had a rough week.

Linda: What happened?

Jerry: Well, I usually like to **bury my head in the sand** and not pay attention to **office gossip** but Tim **stabbed someone in the back**.

Linda: Who?

Jerry: It was his boss.

Linda: Oh wow! Well, **let the dust settle**. I'm sure they won't be like **two peas in a pod** but hopefully, they can **put it behind** them. And surely he won't **get off scot-free**?

Jerry: Tim isn't known for **letting bygones be bygones** so he'll **go down swinging** for sure. I'm honestly just **counting the days** until this **blows over**.

Vocabulary

Stabbed someone in the back: To betray someone, especially someone with a close relationship.

Bury my head in the sand: To avoid a certain situation or problem.

Let the dust settle: Wait for and let a situation become calm or normal after something exciting or unusual happened.

Two peas in a pod: Two people who are very similar in thinking or appearance.

Put it behind: Overcome, or forget about it.

Office gossip: Talking behind someone's back at work, rumours.

Letting bygones be bygones: Putting something behind you, forgiving.

Go down swinging: To continue to fight.

Counting the days: Waiting for something to be finished.

Blows over: A bad time passes or is finished.

Get off scot-free: Not get in trouble for something.

Exercise

Fill in the blanks with the correct phrase or idiom.

1. My sister and I were like _____ growing up.
2. I actively try to avoid _____.
3. I think you two can get back together. Just _____ for a bit.
4. One of the only things I regret in life is the time that I _____.
5. I know it sounds crazy, but I can't let it go and _____ me.
6. If I get fired, I'm going to _____.
7. I don't want to but I tend to _____ and not get involved with conflict.
8. It's really impressive how good my mom is at _____.
9. I hope this _____ quickly. I'm so tired of the drama.
10. I'm _____ until I can retire. I hate my job.
11. How could he honestly expect to _____ after what he did?

Answers:

1. two peas in a pod
2. office gossip
3. let the dust settle
4. stabbed someone in the back
5. put it behind
6. go down swinging
7. bury my head in the sand
8. letting bygones be bygones
9. blows over
10. counting the days
11. get off scot-free

Apologizing to a Co-worker

Tim: **My bad**. Sorry for not finishing my part of the project on time. We're **in hot water** now.

Carrie: You put us in **a tough spot.** Your part is critical to avoid a **bottleneck** for the entire team.

Tim: I'm sorry. How can I make it up to you?

Carrie: I think if you finish your part by tomorrow morning, we can still have it to Jerry on time.

Tim: Okay. I'll **bite the bullet** and won't sleep until it's done.

Carrie: Okay, you know I'd love to help you **crunch the numbers** but **my hands are tied.** I don't have the qualification for that yet.

Tim: No problem. Back to work! Sorry for **dropping the ball** on this.

Carrie: It sounds like we're **on the same page** now. **Keep your eye on the prize**!

Vocabulary

My bad: It's my fault.

In hot water: In trouble.

A tough spot: A bad situation.

Bottleneck: Something that stops the flow. In this case, the project can't continue.

Bite the bullet: Resolve to do something difficult.

Crunch the numbers: Analyze data

My hands are tied: Unable to do something, even if you wanted to.

Dropping the ball: Not getting something done, or doing a bad job.

On the same page: Share a similar way of thinking.

Keep your eye on the prize: Remember the end goal.

Exercise

Fill in the blanks with the correct phrase or idiom.

1. Seriously, _____. Sorry that I didn't get that done in time.
2. I was in _____ when I lost my job.
3. We're going to be _____ if we can't get this done on time.
4. I'm nervous about _____ on this project. My job depends on it.
5. Can you please _____ again? I think there was a mistake somewhere.
6. We need to figure out where the _____ is and get things moving more quickly.
7. You're going to have to _____ and work this weekend.
8. I'd help you if I could but _____.
9. As long as we are _____, I think we'll get along just fine.
10. Whatever happens, make sure you _____.

Answers:

1. my bad
2. a tough spot
3. in hot water
4. dropping the ball
5. crunch the numbers
6. bottleneck
7. bite the bullet
8. my hands are tied
9. on the same page
10. keep your eye on the prize

Talking about a Company in Trouble

Jerry: My company has been **cutting corners** on this latest project and we're **in hot water**.

Linda: Well, honestly, it's time for your company to **face the music.** You've been doing some things that **cross the line** for years now. It's going to be **an uphill battle** for you.

Jerry: Hey, hey. I know. You're **barking up the wrong tree**! I don't have anything to do with making the decisions. I do what I'm told. I'm basically a **yes man.**

Linda: I know. But, I wish you'd find some **greener pastures**. That company is going to **go under** soon I think. Just **read between the lines**.

Jerry: Well, jobs in my field are like a **needle in a haystack** these days. I'd **pull the plug** if I could.

Vocabulary

Cutting Corners: Doing something cheaply or badly. Can often be related to construction/home renovations.

Face the music: Deal with the reality of something negative that you did. For example, getting punished for a crime.

In hot water: In trouble for something.

Cross the line: Behave in an unacceptable way.

Barking up the wrong tree: Blaming someone for something that isn't their fault.

Greener pastures: A better opportunity someplace else.

Go under: Go bankrupt or out of business.

Yes man: A weak person who always agrees with their superior at work or in politics.

Needle in a haystack: Something that is impossible to find.

An uphill battle: Something very difficult to deal with.

Read between the lines: Discovering something secret or hidden.

Pull the plug: Quit, or stop doing something.

Exercise

Fill in the blanks with the correct phrase or idiom.

1. That CEO made some terrible decisions and his company is about to _____.
2. I know you don't want to _____ but your company is about to go bankrupt.
3. I'm leaving my job and heading for _____.
4. It's time to _____ for ripping all those customers off.
5. Honestly, you're _____. Johnny did it, not me.
6. Donald Trump is _____ these days with the most recent scandal.
7. The guy painting my house is _____. I feel so angry about it.
8. I hate that my company likes to _____ on just about every deal they do.
9. I hate that my husband is forced into being a _____ in his new role at the company.
10. Looking for my glasses in my messy house is like finding a _____.
11. Quite honestly, it's going to be _____ to get back on track.
12. I think he's going to _____. That new guy just isn't performing well.

Answers:

1. go under
2. read between the lines
3. greener pastures
4. face the music
5. barking up the wrong tree
6. in hot water
7. cutting corners
8. cross the line
9. yes man
10. needle in a haystack
11. an uphill battle
12. pull the plug

Leaving a Job

Jerry: I'm worried about my job. A **storm is brewing** at my company. They were **let off the hook** last time but I'm not sure the other company won't sue for **breach of contract** this time.

Linda: I mean, **it takes two to tango**. That other company should have seen the **writing on the wall** way earlier than now. Your company missed so many deadlines.

Jerry: I know, it's **an impossible task.** I did my best but it's not going to be enough.

Linda: **Ditch that sinking ship**. Time to move onto bigger and better things and test the waters. Someone will **snap you up** in seconds.

Jerry: You're right. I'm **working my connections** already to **see what's out there**. But **warts and all**, I honestly don't mind working here.

Vocabulary

Let off the hook: To not be punished, even though he/she was caught doing something wrong. For example, a politician who doesn't go to jail even though he committed a crime.

A storm is brewing: Difficulty or danger is expected in the future.

It takes two to tango: There are two people responsible for a situation or problem.

Breach of contract: Breaking the terms in a contract.

Writing on the wall: A sign that something bad is about to happen.

An impossible task: Something that isn't able to be completed.

Ditch that sinking ship: To leave a bad situation.

Snap you up: Hire quickly.

Test the waters: Try something out before committing fully to it.

Working my connections: Talking to people you know to get something from them.

Warts and all: Including things that aren't attractive.

See what's out there: To look for new opportunities.

Exercise

Fill in the blanks with the correct phrase or idiom.

1. Maybe it's just me but I predict that _____ at work.
2. I quit before I could get fired because I saw the _____.
3. I know you're worried about losing your job but someone will _____ so quickly!
4. I couldn't believe that my son was _____ for that thing he did at school. Lucky guy.
5. Well, it's partly my fault but _____.
6. Honestly, that was _____ and not even Superman could have finished it.
7. It's time to _____ and find a better job.
8. That company often doesn't keep its word, but I didn't think a _____ would happen.
9. I'm going to start _____ to hopefully get an internship opportunity.
10. I'm not really looking for a new job but I'm going to _____.
11. I love him, _____.
12. Is it possible to _____ before deciding?

Answers:

1. a storm is brewing
2. writing on the wall
3. snap you up
4. let off the hook
5. it takes two to tango
6. an impossible task
7. ditch that sinking ship
8. breach of contract
9. working my connections
10. see what's out there
11. warts and all
12. test the waters

Talking about Finishing Work for the Day

Jerry: I'm so tired. Let's **call it a day** and grab some dinner. It's **my treat**.

Linda: Sure, I'd love to but only if we **go Dutch**. You **foot the bill** for me too often!

Jerry: Sure, if you insist. Let's check out that dessert place. They have sandwiches and then I can satisfy my **sweet tooth**. It's expensive but **worth it** I think.

Linda: Okay, **twist my arm**. Let's go. And don't just pick up the bill when I'm in the bathroom. I want to **pony up** for my share, okay?

Jerry: Let's **make a break for it** before **the big cheese** finds more work for us to do!

Linda: Sure, let's **head out**.

Vocabulary

Call it a day: To stop working for the rest of the day.

Foot the bill: To pay for.

Go Dutch: Each person pays their own bill, especially at a restaurant or bar.

Pony up: To get money/credit cards out to pay for something.

Worth it: Good enough to justify the high cost.

Twist my arm: Convince to do something.

Sweet tooth: To like sugary foods.

My treat: To offer to pay, usually for a meal or drink.

Make a break for it: Leave somewhere quickly.

The big cheese: The boss.

Head out: To go somewhere.

Exercise

Fill in the blanks with the correct phrase or idiom.

1. I feel uncomfortable when guys pay for me so I insist that we _____.

2. It's time to _____ for all those drinks you had!

3. I have a wicked _____ and can't stop eating candy.

4. Is the company going to _____ for the Christmas party this year?

5. Let's _____. I'm beat.

6. It's time to _____ and go home while the boss isn't looking.

7. Let's grab lunch. _____.

8. I hope to be _____ one day!

9. I'm tired. I'm going to _____ now.

10. Okay, I know that subscription box is expensive but it's _____ to me.

11. I didn't want to do it! My wife had to _____ to get me to go skydiving with her.

Answers:

1. go Dutch

2. pony up

3. sweet tooth

4. foot the bill

5. call it a day

6. make a break for it

7. my treat

8. the big cheese

9. head out

10. worth it

11. twist my arm

Inviting a Co-worker for a Drink

Jerry: Okay, fine Linda, **twist my arm**. I'll go get a drink with you.

Linda: Wait, what? You want to grab a drink? Sure, why not. I'd love to **unwind.**

Jerry: Yeah, I'm having a rough time. I just found out that Braden **got a kickback** on this latest contract. Some bad stuff is **going down**. Our company has certainly **seen better days**.

Linda: Oh wow. That's not good. Let's **kick back and relax**. I know a new place that has some great **craft beer**. We can **talk shop**. Your **secrets are safe with me**.

Jerry: Yeah, it's just the **tip of the iceberg**. A whole bunch of money **vanished into thin air**.

Linda: Oh, wow Jerry! You need to **take a breather**. Meet you at Brown's Pub in 20!

Vocabulary

Twist my arm: Convince someone to do something.

Got a kickback: Accepted a bribe.

Tip of the iceberg: A very small part of something much bigger, usually a negative thing or a problem.

Vanished into thin air: Disappeared without a trace.

Going down: Happening.

Seen better days: In poor/bad condition.

Talk shop: Talk about work with a co-worker.

Your secrets are safe with me: Promise to keep things confidential.

Unwind: Relax.

Kick back and relax: Chill out.

Craft beer: Specialty beer that is brewed in small batches.

Take a breather: Relax for a while.

Exercise

Fill in the blanks with the correct phrase or idiom.

1. There's some crazy stuff _____ in the US election.
2. I can't believe your friend just _____.
3. The politician _____ for awarding the contract to a certain company.
4. Well, that's just the _____. There's a whole lot more that we don't know yet.
5. Okay Joe, you don't have to _____. I'll do it.
6. I used to drink _____ but it's too expensive now that I've lost my job!
7. I'm wondering if his company has _____?
8. I like to watch some Netflix to _____ from the week.
9. My dad loves to _____ with a nice beer on Friday nights.
10. Let's go outside and _____.
11. Please don't _____ tonight, okay? It's so boring!
12. It's okay! Just talk to me. _____.

Answers:

1. going down
2. vanished into thin air
3. got a kickback
4. tip of the iceberg
5. twist my arm
6. craft beer
7. seen better days
8. unwind/kick back and relax
9. unwind/kick back and relax
10. take a breather
11. talk shop
12. your secrets are safe with me

Going Out for Lunch #1

Tom: So how's the **bull market** treating you these days Jenny?

Jenny: Business is **booming** and we'll be even busier in the next few weeks. We **fast-tracked** this new project and are trying to **hit the ground running** with the latest technology. We hope to **corner the market** before our competitors come up with similar products.

Tom: It sounds like you're really **in the driver's seat**.

Jenny: Well we're **walking a tightrope**. Regulators could **pull the plug** at any time and we've already **spent a fortune** on development.

Waiter: Hi, can I get you something to drink?

Jenny: I'd love a glass of red wine and we're ready to order too.

Waiter: Sure, what would you like?

Jenny: I'll have the lasagna, please.

Tom: And I'll have the chicken penne with cream sauce and a glass of your house white.

Waiter: Sure, I'll bring those drinks right out.

Vocabulary

Bull market: When share prices are rising in the stock market.

Booming: Growing or expanding rapidly.

Fast-tracked: Made progress more quickly than normal.

Hit the ground running: Start something and make progress quickly on it.

Corner the market: Gain a lot of the market share.

Driver's seat: In control of something.

Walking a tightrope: To do something that requires extreme care and precision; to navigate a situation that allows for no error.

Pull the plug: To end or finish something, usually suddenly and without warning.

Spent a fortune: To spend a lot of money.

Exercise

Fill in the blanks with the correct phrase or idiom.

1. I hope my boss doesn't _____ on this project. I'm having a lot of fun working on it.
2. We're doing well these days and business is _____.
3. Do you think Samsung's new phone will _____?
4. It's best to sell stocks in a _____ and buy in a bear market.
5. I need a new car but I don't want to _____.
6. We're _____ when dealing with the local regulators.
7. Our company is in the _____ with our latest innovation.
8. My hope is that with that new guy we just hired, we can _____.
9. The project I'm working on got _____ and I'll have to do lots of overtime in these upcoming weeks.

Answers:

1. pull the plug
2. booming
3. corner the market
4. bull market
5. spend a fortune
6. walking a tightrope
7. driver's seat
8. hit the ground running
9. fast-tracked

Going out for Lunch #2

Carrie: How's business these days?

Tom: Well, our **shareholders** are happy but **behind the scenes**, it's pretty chaotic.

Carrie: I know you can't tell me much but **in a nutshell**, what's going on?

Tom: Well, we're **caught between a rock and a hard place** with this latest project. Our competition is so **cutthroat** on their pricing that we've had to **cut corners**.

Carrie: Hopefully you'll **bounce back**. Will you **break even**?

Tom: My **gut feeling** is that it'll happen only if we **go for broke**.

Waiter: Are you ready to order?

Carrie: Not quite yet. Can you give us another minute? I haven't looked at the menu!

Vocabulary

Shareholders: People who hold shares in a company.

Behind the scenes: What happens out of sight from the public.

In a nutshell: A quick summary of something.

Caught between a rock and a hard place: A difficult decision with two or more not ideal options.

Cutthroat: Competitive, fierce, ruthless.

Cut corners: To do something cheaply and easily by ignoring rules or best practices.

Bounce back: To recover after something bad happened.

Break even: Not making money but not losing money.

Gut feeling: An immediate feeling about something, not based on reason or rationality.

Go for broke: To risk everything in one final effort or push.

Exercise

Fill in the blanks with the correct phrase or idiom.

1. My boss thinks that we need to _____ but I don't think things are that bad.
2. That guy is so _____. I hate working for him.
3. Customers are happy but _____, the employees hate working here.
4. I'm hoping my Dad can _____ after he gets home from the hospital.
5. My _____ is that we're not going to survive these next few months.
6. I hate having to _____ but it's the only way to turn a profit in this industry.
7. The _____ are demanding that we replace the CEO.
8. I'm hoping to just _____ this quarter.
9. Being the boss often means that you're _____.
10. _____, the problem is Tommy! He just doesn't do quality work and I'm always fixing his mistakes.

Answers:

1. go for broke
2. cutthroat
3. behind the scenes
4. bounce back
5. gut feeling
6. cut corners
7. shareholders
8. break even
9. caught between a rock and a hard place
10. in a nutshell

Negotiating with Another Company

Ken: I wanted to **touch base** with you and find out where you're at with that new software we recommend to your company.

Bob: Oh you know Jerry. He likes to **take things slowly** and is reluctant to **shake things up**. What we're currently using is fine for now he thinks. Sorry if I gave you **the wrong impression** that this deal might happen quickly.

Ken: To **go out on a limb** here, if you don't upgrade, you'll likely be **playing catch up** for years **down the road**.

Bob: **Big picture**, we know that. Unfortunately, I don't **call the shots** or **hold the purse strings**. Jerry does.

Vocabulary

Touch base: To check in with someone.

Take things slowly: To not move quickly.

Shake things up: To reorganize something in a drastic or big way.

The wrong impression: To think wrongly about someone, based on a first meeting.

Go out on a limb: To take a risk.

Playing catch up: To try to reach the same level as others, especially after starting late.

Down the road: In the future.

Big picture: Considering everything.

Call the shots: To make the decisions.

Hold the purse strings: To make the financial decisions.

Exercise

Fill in the blanks with the correct phrase or idiom.

1. You'll have to talk to Tommy about money stuff. I don't _____.
2. I'm afraid that you've got _____ about our company.
3. Things are fine now but I'm worried about what will happen _____.
4. If we don't upgrade our databases, we'll be _____.
5. I only _____ about HR related things.
6. Can we _____ next week? I'd love to hear how you're doing.
7. My CEO wants to _____ in terms of the kind of people we hire.
8. I don't want to _____ too much here, but someone has to tell you this.
9. I'm a mover and shaker but my boss likes to _____.
10. I know you don't agree with me but I don't think you're looking at the _____.

Answers:

1. hold the purse strings
2. the wrong impression
3. down the road
4. playing catch up
5. call the shots
6. touch base
7. shake things up
8. go out on a limb
9. take things slowly
10. big picture

Talking about a Project

Jerry: I have to **hit the sack.** I'm so tired right now.

Linda: Have you been **burning the midnight oil** lately?

Jerry: Yeah, I've been trying to finish preparing for this big presentation. I got a slow start working on it because I was in the hospital for a few days. It's a **race against the clock** now.

Linda: Well, **better late than never.** But, you need to go to bed early and get enough sleep. If you're tired, you won't be able to concentrate.

Jerry: You're right. It was **many moons** ago that I got a decent night's sleep. I have such **a full plate.** Normally, I like to be **ahead of the curve** on this stuff.

Linda: **Keep fighting**! I think you'll **ace** it.

Jerry: Well, here's hoping I **come up trumps**! Time to **knuckle down** and get to work.

Vocabulary

Hit the sack: Go to bed.

Many moons: A long time ago.

Burning the midnight oil: Staying up late working or studying.

Race against the clock: Time is running out to finish something.

Better late than never: Encouragement after getting a late start to something.

A full plate: Lots to do.

Ahead of the curve: Preparing early for something.

Keep fighting: Keep trying.

Ace: To get a high mark on a test or do well at something like a job interview.

Come up trumps: To get exactly what is needed at the last minute.

Knuckle down: To focus deeply on something.

Exercise

Fill in the blanks with the correct phrase or idiom.

1. Don't forget to _____ early. It's your big game tomorrow!
2. I know it's difficult but ____. Things will get better.
3. Although it was _____ ago, I still think about my ex-boyfriend.
4. I've been _____ lately, working a second job.
5. Honestly, it's _____ but he dropped the ball on this project.
6. You won't _____ the test unless you study.
7. That guy has an uncanny ability to always _____.
8. It's the last thing I want to do but I know it's time to _____ and study.
9. It's going to be a _____ to get this project done.
10. My boss always has _____. He needs to hire more people.
11. I have a master calendar with all my projects so I can stay _____.

Answers:

1. hit the sack
2. keep fighting
3. many moons
4. burning the midnight oil
5. better late than never
6. ace
7. come up trumps
8. knuckle down
9. race against the clock
10. a full plate
11. ahead of the curve

Job Interview

Interviewer: I'm wondering why you're leaving your current position?

Ken: **The cat's out of the bag** so I'm comfortable telling you, but ABC traders are **closing up shop**. They've been struggling to **keep their head above water** for the past year or so.

Interviewer: Oh, wow! I'm **out of the loop**! I get it. I was **in the same boat** once early on in my career.

Ken: That's why I'd love to **get my foot in the door** here. I've heard great things about your **state of the art** technology and that kind of thing is **second nature** to me.

Interviewer: We certainly are **ahead of the pack** when compared to our competitors. We have some **groundbreaking** developments in this industry.

Ken: I'm confident that I can **learn the ropes** and **get up to speed** quickly.

Vocabulary

The cat's out of the bag: Something is no longer a secret.

Closing up shop: Going bankrupt or shutting down.

Keep their head above water: Trying to just break even.

Out of the loop: Don't have some certain information about something.

In the same boat: In a similar situation.

Get my foot in the door: Achieve some initial stage. For example, an entry-level job at a company.

State of the art: Advanced technology.

Second nature: Instinctive, easy to do.

Ahead of the pack: To be ahead of other people or companies trying to do a similar thing.

Groundbreaking: Innovative or new.

Learn the ropes: Get trained to do something.

Get up to speed: Achieve competence.

Exercise

Fill in the blanks with the correct phrase or idiom.

1. I hope it doesn't take me too long to _____ with this new software.
2. I'm looking forward to the _____ software at this new job.
3. Our goal this year is to get _____ with voice recognition software.
4. You and I are _____ here!
5. I'm worried that my company is considering _____.
6. It might take you a while to _____ but I'm confident you'll get it!
7. Back in the day, it was considered to be _____.
8. I'm okay talking about it now that _____.
9. Running these kinds of seminars is _____ to me.
10. I'm willing to do any job just to _____ there.
11. Let's keep Tony _____ on this, okay?
12. That company has to work so hard just to _____.

Answers:

1. get up to speed
2. state of the art
3. ahead of the pack
4. in the same boat

5. closing up shop

6. learn the ropes

7. groundbreaking

8. the cat's out of the bag

9. second nature

10. get my foot in the door

11. out of the loop

12. keep their head above water

Before You Go

If you found this book useful, please leave a review wherever you bought it. It will help other English learners, like yourself find this resource.

You might also be interested in this book: _Advanced English Conversation Dialogues_ by Jackie Bolen. It has hundreds of helpful English idioms and expressions. Learn to speak more fluently in American English.

CPSIA information can be obtained
at www.ICGtesting.com
Printed in the USA
LVHW020632280422
717240LV00016B/1583